This Coloring Book Belongs To

_____

_____

COLORING BOOK FOR CHILDREN'S

- Acknowledgement -

Thank you for purchasing this coloring book,

We hope you have a fun, relaxing, and wonderful experience when coloring.

A special thanks to our online community for providing feedback, support, and for sharing

your beautiful colored pages for everyone to enjoy. You inspire our team every day.

Copyright @ 2024 The Staging Lanes LLC
AND B&B BOOKS
All Rights Reserved

- No Grayscale Coloring Pages -

There is no Grayscale, Every image having plenty of space

for artists to express their creativity with color.

Made in United States
Orlando, FL
07 December 2024

55099451R00057